# TAKE A
# HIKE
**WITH YOUR CHILDREN**™

Featuring Hikes of 5K or Less in
Banff, Canmore, Kananaskis and Lake Louise

# By Lynda Pianosi

Getting Families Closer to Nature One Step at a Time™

*Take a Hike with Your Children*<sup>TM</sup> *from Tots to Tweens in the Canadian Rockies: Featuring Hikes of 5K or Less in Banff, Canmore, Kananaskis, and Lake Louise*

Three Mountain Family Hikes<sup>TM</sup>

For information, contact the publisher at:

Pianosi Publishing

Box 8329

Canmore AB  T1W 2V1

Lynda@takeahikewithyourchildren.ca

Visit our website at www.takeahikewithyourchildren.ca

First edition published: 2011

Second Printing 2012

Third Printing 2013

Fourth Printing 2014

Fifth Printing 2015

Sixth Printing 2017

Seventh Printing 2018

Credits: Stefanie Procee, illustrator; John Breeze, book design & layout; Natalie Chin, Cover design. All of the photographs used in this book were taken by the Author.

PRINTED AND BOUND IN CANADA

ISBN: 978-0-9867020-0-6

# Testimonials

*Living in the Lake Louise/Banff area for the past 30 years and raising our three children in the mountain park, we've experienced many, if not most, of the walks and hikes described in this book. I've come to notice many families at a loss to find suitable activities (outside of shopping and eating on Banff Avenue) and missing out on an opportunity to experience the true nature of our natural treasure. This book offers a very valuable tool for all those, young and old, hoping to spend a pleasant day or two in a truly awesome setting. Not to be missed.*

Elaine Tessolini, physiotherapist

*This book is an easy to use, icon-based, hiking guide for families, inspired from Lynda's own experiences with her family out on the trails. This means our author has gone before us. She has done the hikes, taken that wrong turn, forgot to have a Plan B, and yes, sprayed the bear spray up wind, (for which her children are always quick to remind her). For us, the reader, this makes for a "best-practices" trail guide. Fun and easy to use, this manual is aimed at helping families have a great day out on the trails. Thank you, Lynda!*

Marcus Horeak, Former Columnist & Writer for "Pedal" Magazine, Canada's National Cycling magazine

*This book is an easy read and well written. It provides the essential information one would like to know such as the difficulty level of the hiking trails in this book, designed for the entire family from beginner trails to the more advanced. I recommend this book as family hikes can be a good form of physical activity and an excellent form of social support, which are two of many key elements that are important to a healthy lifestyle."*

Dr. Conrad Tang, Sports Chiropractor

## Disclaimer

The author designed the information to represent her opinions about the subjects disclosed. The reader must weigh carefully all aspects of any personal decisions before undertaking any of the suggestions in this book. The author obtained the information contained through research and life experience.

The author speaks from her perspective and disclaims any liability, loss or risk incurred by individuals who act on the information enclosed. The author believes the information and advice presented here is sound, but readers cannot hold Lynda Pianosi and/or Pianosi Publishing responsible for any actions they take as a result of this book.

## Dedication

- To my two sons, who claim they have walked "at least a million miles" doing these hikes. My sons were the best critics and barometers for the hikes and Plan B's that I have included in this book.
- To my husband for his encouragement to write the book, and for pushing the Chariot up and down the trail while our boys both sat comfortably inside.
- To my dad for instilling in me a love for the outdoors, which started at a very young age and is a part of who I am today.
- To both of my parents for their following words of wisdom: "Get outside and play; you're wasting a beautiful day indoors." Something I still do, hence the reason for my messy house!

## Acknowledgements

I would like to thank Conrad, Elaine, Marcus, Stella and John for their proof reading, editing and words of encouragement.

## Foreword

### By Marcus Horeak

Lynda loves sharing with children her passions for the outdoors that she developed with her parents as a young child growing up in rural Ontario. Coming full circle, Lynda now watches the excitement of her own two boys who love getting out of the house to hike and bike.  And watching her boys make their own discoveries in life outside, away from the cities and computers that seem to be in every corner of our lives these days, has ignited a spark she wants to share with other families.

"When I was looking for books on easy hikes for families with young children," Lynda says. "There wasn't one. When I complained to my husband, he said, 'Why don't you write one.' So I did!"

This book is an easy to use, icon-based, hiking guide for families, inspired from Lynda's own experiences with her family out on the trails.  This means our author has gone before us.  She had done the hikes, taken that wrong turn, forgot to have a Plan B, and yes, sprayed the bear spray up wind, (for which her children are always quick to remind her). For us, the reader, this makes for a "best-practices" trail guide.  Fun and easy to use, this manual is aimed at helping families have a great day out on the trails.  Thank you, Lynda!

# Table of Contents

## 1 Introduction

he purpose of this book is to get families active, outside
nd interested in nature.

The benefits are

- With the exception of four hikes that have a special
  attraction, all hikes in this book are 5 kilometres or less
  in length and, therefore, very much "doable" for young
  families or families that have a mix of infants to tweens.

- There are more than 40 hikes within a two-hour drive
  from Calgary.

- ❖ There is a Plan B for all hikes, as parents, we all know
  that the best plans can result in changes due to weather
  or children's moods. So for each hike there are several
  alternatives, such as a playground or an interpretive
  centre to visit, rather than do the hike.

- The book doesn't go into a lot of extra detail about the
  flora and fauna of the hikes because, as parents with
  young children, we don't always have the extra time to
  read these details.

- There are no fees required to access any of the hikes in
  this book (but you do need a valid pass to be in the
  National Parks, of course).

There are two "Additional Hikes" described at the end of
this book. Located near Cochrane, they are ideal
destinations for short day trips with the kids.

# 2 The Icons—What they Mean

| | |
|---|---|
| | *All-terrain stroller* – preferably one with large wheels that can make it over rough, uneven ground |
| | *Bathrooms* – flush toilets, running water (not necessarily hot) |
| | *Benches* – benches available for resting |
| | *Child pack carriers* – either a front or back carrier |
| | *Fire pits and/or barbeques* – designated areas for fires/barbeques but only when there isn't a fire ban in effect |
| | *Firewood* - provided by the parks and available at the hike location for use in the designated fire pits |
| | *Picnic shelters* – covered buildings with picnic tables inside |
| | *Picnic tables* – picnic tables without shelters |
| | *Sun* – trail is in full sun, no shade |
| | *Sun/shade* – the trail is in a mix of sun and shade |
| | *Vault toilets*- outhouse style toilets |

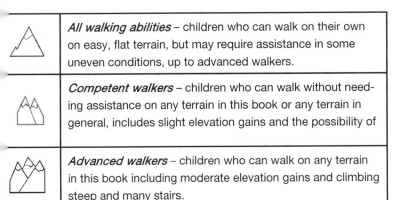

| | |
|---|---|
| | *All walking abilities* – children who can walk on their own on easy, flat terrain, but may require assistance in some uneven conditions, up to advanced walkers. |
| | *Competent walkers* – children who can walk without needing assistance on any terrain in this book or any terrain in general, includes slight elevation gains and the possibility of |
| | *Advanced walkers* – children who can walk on any terrain in this book including moderate elevation gains and climbing steep and many stairs. |

arents are the best judge of their children's walking abilities, the definitions for all walking abilities, competent and dvanced walkers should be used as guidelines only.

## 3 First Aid

A basic first aid kit is a must for any outing. A variety of first aid kits that range from basic to advanced can be purchased at local shops. Price ranges of pre-made kits vary depending upon the content and size of the kit. It is also possible to create your own custom made kit and there are many websites available to provide you with that information. Don't forget bug spray and sun screen!

# 4 Dressing for the Mountains

The weather in the mountains can change as quickly as a toddler's attention span. Therefore, it is imperative to bring along clothing items that you might not need at the outset of your trip. Rain gear, warm clothes and a change of clothes, as well as, yes, sometimes even mittens for little hands in the late summer or early spring. Of course these same items should be brought along for mom and dad as well.

Now more than ever before, being sun smart is important. A good hat is a must, ideally with an SPF rating for the summer. Try to ensure that the sun hats have a large brim that generously cover the eyes and back of the neck. Winter hats may be necessary for early spring and late summer hikes. Sunglasses are a great idea for any time of the year.

Keep in mind that you are in the mountains, so even though it is sunny and warm at the bottom of the trail, the gain in elevation can lead to cooler temperatures at the top.

## 5 Your Eco-footprint

This is defined, by one of my sons, as "how hard Mother Nature needs to work to support us." Everything we do, the food choices we make, the method of transportation we use, the way we choose to dispose of our household garbage affects the environment. For example, if you wander off the designated trail while on your hike, you could be causing a negative impact on the grasses and plants that you step on. Other people will see your path and start taking it as well, which over time will cause erosion and negatively impact the area.

Some ways to reduce your Eco Footprint while enjoying nature:

- ❖ Take pictures, not objects. Keep in mind that picking flowers in a National or Provincial Park is illegal.
- ❖ Don't leave anything behind.
- ❖ Stay on the trails.
- ❖ Use the garbage disposals available at the trial heads.
- ❖ Use the washrooms available at the trail heads.

# 6 Yo Bear, Hey Bear, and Other Wildlife

The hikes in this book can be frequented by bears, cougars, elk and other wildlife. It is important to respect this fact and to understand that ALL wild animals, no matter how cute or small, are wild and can be very unpredictable. The Bow Valley Wild*Smart* Community Program, www.bvwildsmart.ca, provides the following important tips when hiking.

To Be Bear Smart
- ❖ Avoid surprise encounters. Loud shouting, our family favourite is "Yo Bear, Hey Bear," or singing is more effective than bear bells.
- ❖ Travel in groups.
- ❖ Carry bear spray or an air horn and know how to use them.
- ❖ Keep your dog on a leash.
- ❖ Leave the area if you see a bear or if you see or smell a dead animal.

If you encounter a Bear:
- ❖ Never run; it may trigger an attack.
- ❖ Slowly back away.
- ❖ Appear passive.

❖ Do not raise your voice or make direct eye contact.

o Be Cougar Smart:
   ❖ Keep your group close together.
   ❖ Keep dogs on a leash.
   ❖ Make noise to alert cougars of your presence.
   ❖ Avoid any area where you find or smell a dead animal, cougars often cover their kills with forest debris.

 you encounter a Cougar:
   ❖ Immediately pick up your children.
   ❖ Maintain eye contact with the cougar.
   ❖ Always leave room for it to escape.
   ❖ Do not turn your back on a cougar. Do not run.
   ❖ Back away slowly. Make yourself appear as large as possible.
   ❖ If a cougar attacks, fight back with anything at hand.

To Be Elk Smart:
   ❖ As passive as they may look, elk can be very aggressive.
   ❖ Do not approach elk or their calves.
   ❖ Keep a distance of at least three bus lengths.
   ❖ Keep your dog on a leash.

If you encounter an Elk:

- ❖ Hide behind a large structure such as a car, tree, outhouse.
- ❖ Use your bear spray.

Other Wildlife

- ❖ Be respectful of all wildlife. Many of the smaller animals have associated humans with food, therefore it isn't uncommon to see a Richardson Ground Squirrel approach an outstretched hand in hope of a "treat".
- ❖ Feeding wildlife is illegal and it creates a wide range of problems for wild animals*

* See Feeding Wildlife at www.Watertonpark.com

# 7 How to "PP" in the Woods

s parents, we have all asked "are you sure you don't need
ɔ go?" and, of course, within the first five minutes of your
ike, Murphy's Law will kick in.  It isn't a matter of if, but
vhen this will happen and, when it does, here are some tips
ɔ help you be prepared:

ind a secluded place behind a tree or rock that is not too
lose to the trail and make sure you are at least 200 feet
ɾom any water source.

ɔllow the golden rule: pack out what you pack in!  This
neans you need to bring extra plastic bags. If you hike with
ɪ family dog, you are already ahead of the game with plastic
ɔags, and, yes, you also need to pack out Fido's mess as
vell.

# Overview of the Banff Hikes

| Hike | Page | (icon 1) | (icon 2) | (icon 3) | (icon 4) | (icon 5) | (icon 6) | (icon 7) | (icon 8) | (icon 9) | (icon 10) | (icon 11) | (icon 12) | (icon 13) | (icon 14) |
|---|---|---|---|---|---|---|---|---|---|---|---|---|---|---|---|
| Bankhead (1.1k interp.loop) | 14 | | X | | | X | | | | | | X | | | X |
| Bow Falls Trail (2.4k return) | 17 | | | X | | X | | | | | | X | X | X | X |
| Bow River Trail (2.3k return) | 20 | | | X | | X | | | | | | X | X | X | X |
| Cascade Ponds (864m loop) | 22 | | | X | X | | | | | | X | X | | | X |
| Cave and Basin Trail (3k return) | 24 | | | X | | X | X | X | X | X | | X | | X | X |
| Fenland Trail (2 k loop) | 26 | | | X | X | X | | X | | | | X | X | | X |
| Johnson Lake (3k loop) | 29 | | X | X† | X | X | | | | | | X | X | | X* |

† south side of the lake

* single strollers north side only

# Overview of the Banff Hikes

| Hike | Page | 1 | 2 | 3 | 4 | 5 | 6 | 7 | 8 | 9 | 10 | 11 | 12 | 13 | 14 |
|---|---|---|---|---|---|---|---|---|---|---|---|---|---|---|---|
| Johnston Canyon (2.2k return to Lower Falls; 4.8k return to Upper Falls) | 32 | | ✖ | | | ✖ | | | | | | ✖ | ✖ | | ✖* |
| Marsh Loop (2.3k) | 35 | | | ✖ | | ✖ | | | | | | ✖ | | | ✖ |
| Marsh Trail Boardwalk (500m loop) | 38 | | ✖ | | | ✖ | | | | | | ✖ | ✖ | ✖ | ✖ |
| Stewart Canyon (3.4k return) | 41 | | ✖ | | ✖ | ✖ | | ✖ | ✖ | | ✖ | ✖ | ✖ | ✖ | ✖* |
| Tunnel Mountain Hoodoos Interpretive Trail (k return) | 43 | | ✖ | | ✖ | | ✖ | | | | | ✖ | ✖ | | ✖ |
| Tunnel Mountain (3k return) | 45 | ✖ | | | | ✖ | | | | | | ✖ | | | ✖ |

* single strollers only

## Plan B Alternatives for Banff Hikes

### *Banff Central Park*
This park is very close to the main street of Banff. There is no play apparatus, but this park does provide a great spot for a picnic, although shade is limited. There is a full-service bathroom. Take Highway 1 to Banff/Lake Minnewanka turn-off, turn south towards the town of Banff and head south on Banff Avenue to Buffalo Street.

### *Banff Recreation Grounds*
This is a great park for children of all ages. There are bathrooms, picnic tables, picnic shelters and barbeques. To get there take Banff Avenue south, cross the bridge and turn west onto Cave Avenue. Then turn north onto Birch Crescent and west onto Birch Avenue.

### *Banff Rotary Park*
This is a well-shaded park that offers play apparatus for children twelve and under. There are picnic tables but no washroom facilities. It is located at the corner of Banff Avenue and Marmot Crescent.

### *Lake Minnewanka*
Hang out, throw stones in the water, have a picnic. Take Highway 1 to the Banff/Lake Minnewanka Loop. Once on the Minnewanka Road, the sign is just "Lake Minnewanka." Continue following the signs to Lake Minnewanka.

## Bankhead – 1.1K Interpretive Loop

### What?

This 1.1K interpretive loop takes you past the remains of the once lively and economically viable town site of Bankhead. Coal was mined here, but the town site closed down in the late 1920s. The presence of coal is still very evident as you walk along the blackened pathways. The interpretive signs do stress a health caution about the remaining coal tar and suggest that you do not pick-up any of the stones nor pick any rhubarb left from the once flourishing gardens. You are cautioned not to "explore" the existing buildings, as the foundations of these are not safe. Despite all these

## Bankhead ...

warnings, it is still a
very interesting and
easy family hike.
There are 76 stairs
and five landings
where you will need to
carry a stroller down
and then up when you
return.

### Who?
All-terrain stroller,
child pack carriers,
competent and
advanced walkers.

### When?
Any time of day as
both trail options have
a mix of sun and
shade.

### Where?
Take Highway 1 to the Banff/Lake Minnewanka Loop. Once
on the Minnewanka Road, the sign is just "Lake
Minnewanka." Continue following the signs to Lake
Minnewanka. Go past the turn-offs for Cascade Ponds,
Two-Jake Lake and Johnson Canyon. Just after the Granite

**Bankhead ...**

War Memorial, turn right into the Bankhead parking lot.

**Plan B** – See Page 13.

## Bow Falls Trail – 2.4K Return

## What?

This easy 2.4K return trail follows the Bow River and provides a picturesque view of the Bow Falls from the pathway. Advanced Walkers can explore a set of over 100 stairs which ascend and descend above the falls, providing different vantage points. The pathway across the top portion of the falls is relatively flat, and is accessible for any walking ability. Portions of this pathway are shared with horseback riders and bikers, so be alert and courteous to

## Bow Falls Trail ...

the horses.

### Who?
All walking
abilities, all-
terrain strollers,
child pack
carriers.

### When?
Any time of day as the trail is a mix of sun and shade.

### Where?
### Option 1: Bow Falls Parking Lot
Take Highway 1 to Banff/Lake Minnewanka turn-off, turn
south towards the town of Banff and head south on Banff
Avenue to Spray Avenue. Cross over the bridge and turn
east onto Spray Avenue and follow the signs to the Banff

Springs Hotel. Turn
left at the Bow Falls
Road which then
turns into Bow Falls
Avenue and follow
the signs to the
parking lot.

### Option 2: Central

**Bow Falls Trail ...**

## Park

Take Highway 1 to Banff/Lake Minnewanka turn-off, turn south towards the town of Banff and head south on Banff Avenue to Buffalo Street. Pick up the trail just behind the Museum. You will need to cross Banff Avenue either at the lights or looping around and under the bridge. The Bow Falls Trail is on the south side of the river and you can pick it up again just by the YWCA.

**Plan B** – See Page 13.

## Bow River Trail – 2.3K Return

### What?

This is an easy 2.3K return trail, on a wheelchair accessible pathway, that meanders along the brilliant blue Bow River. It has a majestic 360 degree view of the mountains among which the town of Banff is nestled. The trail is clearly marked and is very popular during the summer months. Central Park is a great place to stop for a rest or a picnic before you continue along your way. Alternatively, you could park at Central Park and start the trail from here.

## Bow River Trail ...

### Who?
All walking abilities, all-terrain strollers, child pack carriers.

### When?
Any time of day as both trail options have a mix of sun and shade.

### Where?
**Option 1:** Highway 1 to the Banff/Mount Norquay Road turn-off. Head south on Mount Norquay Road, which will turn into Lynx Street. Turn west at Wolf Street. The trail head starts at the *Blue Canoe* rental booth.

**Option 2:** Central Park

Take Highway 1 to Banff/Lake Minnewanka turn-off, turn south towards the town of Banff and head south on Banff Avenue to Buffalo Street. The parking lot is behind the Museum. You can pick up the trail from the parking lot.

Plan B – See Page 13.

# Cascade Ponds – 864 metre loop

## What?

An 864 metre loop that circles the ponds, the path is a combination of pavement and hard-packed gravel with two bridges over the ponds. It is a perfect path for strollers and walkers of all abilities. In addition to the walking trail, you can swim, float in a raft, canoe or play on the shores of the ponds. There are fire pits and two covered picnic shelters available at various locations around the ponds.

## Who?

All walking abilities, all-terrain strollers, child pack carriers.

## Cascade Ponds ...

### When?
There is limited shade on the loop, so the best times to go are early morning or late afternoon.

### Where?
From Highway 1, turn onto the Banff/Minnewanka Loop Road, follow the signs to Lake Minnewanka Loop Road. After the metal grate/Texas Gate in the road, take your first right into the Cascade ponds parking lot.

**Plan B** – See Page 13.

# Cave & Basin Trail – 3 K return

## What?

A very easy, hard-packed trail that takes you through a stand of lodge-pole pines, ending at the Cave and Basin National Historical site. The trail runs parallel to Cave Avenue and the horseback riding trail. From this trail you can get onto the Marsh Trail Loop or the Marsh Boardwalk Loop. You could visit the Cave and Basin National Historical Site and/or reward yourself (and others!) with an ice cream at the café located at this site.

## Cave & Basin Trail ...

### Who?
All walking abilities, all-terrain strollers, child pack carriers.

### When?
Any time of day as the trail has a mix of sun and shade.

### Where?
Take Highway 1 to the Banff/Lake Minnewanka turn-off, turn south towards the town of Banff and head south on Banff Avenue. Cross the bridge and then turn west onto Cave Avenue. Turn north onto Birch Crescent and west onto Birch Avenue. The actual trail starts at the corner of Cave Avenue and Birch Crescent, so it is best to park at the Banff Recreation Grounds parking lot and walk back to the trail.

**Plan B** – See Page 13.

## Fenland Trail – 2K Loop

## What?

This easy 2K, interpretive, looped trail is located on the outskirts of the Banff town site. Self-guided interpretive brochures are available in the parking lot at the start of the trail. After you cross the bridge, you will reach a fork in the trail. Keep left for the Fenland Trail. The name of the trail, "Fenland" refers to a type of wetland which is nourished by nutrient-wet groundwater. During very wet periods, this can mean mosquitoes, so bug repellent is advised. There are benches, bridges and make-shift beaches along the trail,

## Fenland Trail ...

which you can utilize. From many riverbank vantage points you can see canoeists on their way to or from Vermillion Lakes. There are "Log Bridges," which are not recommended for crossing, but these are great for young ones to imagine the forest trolls that might live under them. This trail is close to Banff, but elk and other wildlife frequent this area, so take the necessary precautions.

### Who?
All walking abilities, all-terrain strollers, child pack carriers.

### When?
Any time of day as the trail is a mix of sun and shade.

### Where?
Take Highway 1 to the Banff / Mount Norquay turn-off and go south into Banff. Take the second right into the parking lot. If you go past the "Welcome to Banff" sign, you have

**Fenland Trail ...**

gone too far.

**Plan B** – See Page 13.

## Johnson Lake – 3 K loop

### What?

This is a 3K, looped trail around Johnston Lake. The first 763 metres of the trail along the North side of the lake are stroller accessible. However, there is a short section of the north side of the trail that is very narrow: you can push a single All-Terrain Stroller through this part, but there isn't much room for other people to pass. It is also steep here, and a slip of the foot could result in a tumble into the water. Therefore, this side of the lake is better suited for Competent Walkers or children in backpack carriers. The trail on the south side of the lake is considerably more level, and wider, so it's ideal for all walking levels and for double-wide strollers. Vantage points around the lake offer great

## Johnson Lake ...

views of the Fairholme Benchlands Range, a burnt-out forest, Mount Rundle and the ski runs of Mount Norquay. There are benches situated around the lake and, for the very brave, there is a rope swing on the south side of the lake. Johnson Lake is home to mating loons and if you're lucky you can catch a glimpse of the babies hitching a ride on their parent's back. It is considered to be one of the warmer lakes in the Banff area (although warm is a relative term, particularly if you are a transplanted Ontarian).

### Who?
South Shore - All walking abilities, all-terrain strollers, child pack carriers.
North Shore - Competent and advanced walkers, child Pack carriers, single all-terrain strollers.

### When?
Any time of day as the trail has a mix of sun and shade.

### Where?
Take Highway 1 to the Banff/Lake Minnewanka Loop Road turnoff, drive towards lake Minnewanka, go over the metal grate/Texas Gate and take your second right at the "Two-Jake Camping, Johnson Lake" sign. Follow this road and turn right onto the 'Johnson Lake" turnoff.

### Plan B—Johnson Lake
- *Johnson Lake* - Play at the beach, have a picnic

## Johnson Lake ...

See Page 13– for other ideas.

# Johnston Canyon –
## 2.2K Return (lower falls) 4.8 K Return (upper falls)

## What?

A very popular interpretive hike that meanders through the limestone walls of Johnston Canyon and past seven waterfalls. The first part of the trail is on a suspended walkway that takes you to the lower falls, a 2.2K round trip. The second portion of the trail is a mix of a suspended walkway and pathway to the upper falls, a 4.8K return trip. This hike is popular all year round with mid-summer being the most popular.

## Who?

Competent and advanced walkers, child pack carriers, single all-Terrain strollers can be used but there are some very narrow sections along the suspended walkway which can be difficult to navigate during busy times.

**Johnston Canyon ...**

**When?**
Any time of day as the trail is a mix of sun and shade. Use caution during wet weather as the suspended walkway can get slippery.

**Where?**
There are two options for getting to Johnston Canyon.

*Option 1:* Take Highway 1 to Highway 93 Radium/ Windermere turn-off. Follow the signs towards Castle Junction/ Bow Valley Parkway. Turn right at the junction of Highway 98 and Bow Valley Parkway and backtrack to Johnston Canyon.

*Option 2:* From Bow Valley Parkway, take Highway 1A to Johnston Canyon. This is a very scenic route to Johnston Canyon and Lake Louise. There are many interpretive signs and stops along the way, which describe the ecology, geology and history of this area. There is an abundance of photo opportunities on this route, including mountain landscapes, flowers and wildlife. It is a very popular road for cyclists in the summer months. Due to the possibility of wildlife on the road as well as cyclists you are encouraged to follow the posted speed limits.

Johnston Canyon ...

## Plan B—Johnston Canyon

- ***Johnston Canyon Resort*** - Get some Ice cream.

See Page 13 for other ideas.

## Marsh Loop – 2.3 K loop

### What?

This flat 2.3K loop takes you through a marsh habitat. At one point, the trail meanders beside the Bow River, with several sections that allow easy access to the river for a closer look. If you take the time, you can see footprints left in the muddy river banks from the various animals that have passed along here. This trail is also used by the horseback trail riding companies in Banff: if you encounter a group of riders on the trail, let the horses have right of way. As with

## Marsh Loop ...

all trails in the National Parks, it is also home to the local wildlife that frequents this area, so it's important to make noise while on this trail. On several occasions we have come across elk and their calves, and we have seen fresh bear scat on this particular trail.

### Who?
All walking abilities, all-terrain strollers, child pack carriers.

### When?
Any time of day as the trail has a mix of sun and shade.

## Marsh Loop ...

### Where?
Take Highway 1 to Banff/Lake Minnewanka turn-off, turn south towards the town of Banff and head south on Banff Avenue to Spray Avenue. Cross over the bridge, turn west onto Cave Avenue to the Cave and Basin Historic site parking lot.

### Plan B – See Page 13.

*Take a Hike ... Lynda Pianosi*

## Marsh Trail Boardwalk – 500 metre loop

### What?

This interpretive boardwalk provides great views of the Vermillion Lakes Wetlands and gives information about the fish (such as Mosquito Fish or Jewel Fish), the reptiles (such as garter snakes), the birds (including Lesser Scaups and Red-Winged Blackbirds), and the different species of plants and algae that call this area home. At the end of the boardwalk, a Bird Observation Platform provides opportunities to spot some of the common summer and winter birds that visit this area. A stroller can be pushed along the boardwalk, but there are 40 stairs, separated by

A local resident at
Lake Agnes Teahouse
*(Lake Louise hikes)*

Spring Bonfire at
Cascade Ponds
*(Banff hikes)*

Boulton Creek Trading Post
*(Kananaskis hikes)*

Rawson Lake
*(Kananaskis hikes)*

Plate I

Colour Plates

*Take a Hike ... Lynda Pianosi*

Fall hike in
Larch Valley,
*(Lake Louise hikes)*

Exploring at Lake
Minnewanka,
*(Banff hikes)*

Checking out a Grizzly
Bear dig, Larch Valley
*(Lake Louise hikes)*

View to the NE from
Tunnel Mountain
*(Banff hikes)*

Plate II

View of Upper
Kananaskis Lake from
the trail to Sarrail Falls
*(Kananaskis hikes)*

View of Moraine Lake
from the Rockpile
*(Lake Louise hikes)*

Kananaskis Village kids park

Grassi Lakes Hike,
Option 2, view of the
falls *(Canmore hikes)*

Plate III

Historic Building on
the Bankhead Hike
*(Banff hikes)*

Playing in the Bow
River in Canmore

Mirror Lake and
the Beehive
*(Lake Louise hikes)*

Canmore view from
Grassi Lakes Trail,
Option 2
*(Canmore hikes)*

Plate IV

## Marsh Trail Boardwalk …

three platforms, at different sections along the path. You can leave the stroller at the first platform or, if you are feeling strong, you can carry the stroller down/up the stairs.

On warm sunny days, the start of this trail is a great place to see garter snakes sunning themselves. If you are fortunate enough to see one of these reptiles, remember that it is illegal (and unkind!) to touch them and the best way to preserve a memory is to take a picture.

### Who?
Competent and advanced walkers, all-terrain strollers, child pack carriers.

### When?
Any time of day as the trail is a mix of sun and shade.

### Where?
Take Highway 1 to the Banff/Lake Minnewanka turn-off, turn south towards the town of Banff and head south on Banff Avenue to Spray Avenue. Cross over the

**Marsh Trail Boardwalk ...**

bridge, turn west onto Cave Avenue to the Cave and Basin Historic site parking lot.  Follow the signs to the Cave and Basin Historical Building. The trail starts at the corner of the pool.

**Plan B** – See Page 13.

# Stewart Canyon – 3.4 K return

## What?

This shaded 3.4K return pathway follows the shoreline of Lake Minnewanka to a bridge that spans Stewart Canyon. It is a popular pathway in the summer and is shared between hikers, bikers and back-country campers. Be very careful here with small children! The bridge that spans the canyon is not "childproof": it is very easy for a child to slip between the railings and fall into the canyon. Getting out of the water would be difficult, as the walls of canyon are steep and the water is extremely cold.

*Take a Hike ... Lynda Pianosi*

## Stewart Canyon ...

**Who?**
Competent and advanced walkers, single all-terrain strollers, and child pack carriers. The first 700m is suitable for all walking abilities.

**When?**
Any time of day as the trail has a mix of sun and shade.

**Where?**
Take Highway 1 to the Lake Minnewanka/Banff turnoff. Follow the signs to Lake Minnewanka and arrive at the parking lot. Follow the tarmac sidewalks towards the lake. Walk past the convenience store and follow the signs to Stewart Canyon.

**Plan B** – See Page 13.

# Tunnel Mountain Hoodoos
## Interpretive Trail – 1K return

## What?

The first three-quarters of this paved interpretive pathway is a steady, but easy uphill climb with a rewarding view of the Hoodoos and picturesque views of the Bow River Valley looking towards the town of Banff, the Banff Springs Hotel, Mount Rundle and Tunnel Mountain. The pathway becomes very narrow at times, but it is manageable with a double-wide stroller. You will need to use proper trail etiquette when meeting other people on the trail, i.e. make way for

## Tunnel Mountain Hoodoos ...

others. Also, there are sections of the trail that have some
very steep sides, so exercise caution with young children
along these sections.

**Who?**
Advanced
walkers, all-
terrain strollers,
child pack
carriers.

**When?**
There is limited
shade, so early
morning or late afternoon are the best times to walk this
trail.

**Where?**
Take Highway 1 to Banff/Lake Minnewanka turn-off, turn
south towards the town of Banff and head south on Banff
Avenue. Turn east onto Tunnel Mountain Road. The parking
lot is located across from the Campground.

Plan B – See Page 13.

# Tunnel Mountain – 3 K return

## What?

A 3K return hike that climbs steadily upwards on switchbacks for an elevation gain of 1692 metres. There are some great panoramic views from the top. To the West is a view of the Banff town site, extending to the Vermillion Lakes and continuing along the valley. The Eastern view looks towards Lake Minnewanka and the Fairholme Mountain Range. Exercise caution with children at the top of the Eastern side of Tunnel Mountain, as the viewing area, although spectacular, is situated at the top of a cliff. There

## Tunnel Mountain ...

is a metal railing fence here, but it is not childproof.

Tunnel Mountain is also referred to as The Sleeping Buffalo, as it resembles one when seen from the North and East.

### Who?

Advanced walkers, all-terrain strollers, child pack carriers.

### When?

Any time of day as the trail is a mix of sun and shade. This is a well-worn trail that can be slippery in wet weather.

### Where?

Take Highway 1 to Banff/Lake Minnewanka turn-off; turn south towards the town of Banff and head south on Banff Avenue. Turn onto Tunnel Mountain Road, drive past the camp grounds and turn onto Tunnel Mountain Drive, beside the Douglas Fir Resort. The trail head is located across the road from the parking lot .

Plan B – See Page 13.

# Overview of the Canmore Hikes

| Hike | Page | 🏃‍stroller | 🚰 | 🪵 | 🔭 | | | | 🧺 | ☀️ | 🦌 | 🏷️ | △ | ◁ | ◇ |
|---|---|---|---|---|---|---|---|---|---|---|---|---|---|---|---|
| Bow Loop (1.5 k) | 49 | X | | X | X | | | | X | | X | | X | | |
| Cougar Creek Hike (2k return) | 51 | X | | X | X | | | | | X | | | X | | |
| Grassi Lakes (4 k return) | 53 | | | | | | | | | | | | X (Trail 1) | | X (Trail 2) |
| Grotto Canyon (5 k return) | 56 | | | X | X | | | | | | X | X | | X | |
| Heart Creek Trail (3k return) | 59 | | | X | X | | | | | | X | X | | X | |
| Larch Islands Loop (1.5k) | 61 | X* | | | X | | | | | | X | | X | | |
| Policeman's Creek Boardwalk (.8k return) | 63 | X | | X | X | | | | | X | | | X | | |

* single strollers only

# Plan B – Canmore Hikes

## Centennial Park

This park, situated in downtown Canmore, is great for children of all ages. There are bathrooms, picnic tables and sun/shade. Take Main (Eighth) Street west, turn south on Sixth Avenue, the park is at the end of this road.

## Lions Park

This is a great park for all ages. It offers bathrooms and a mix of sun/shade. Take Main (Eighth) Street west, turn north on Seventh Avenue and follow Seventh Avenue past the pond as it goes over Eighth Avenue and eventually ends at 15th Street. Continue west on 15th street, the park is located at the corner of 15th street and 10th Avenue.

## Eagle Terrace Park

This is a park with play apparatus for all ages, vault toilets; picnic tables, benches. There is minimal shade. Continue on Benchlands Trail, past the Creekside Country Inn, until it turns into Eagle Terrace road. The parking lot for the playground is on the right as you head up the hill.

## Larch Park –

This is a park for toddlers, although older children will also enjoy some of the apparatus. The park is located after you come out at the end of the forested portion of the Larch Loop. There are no bathroom facilities and shade is limited.

## Bow Loop – 1.5K Loop

### What?
This 1.5K, flat, very easy interpretive loop meanders along the Bow River. The pathway takes you over a retired Engine Bridge, built in 1892, and past the TransAlta Rundle Hydro Plant. There are stunning mountain views from every section of this loop. This is a busy path for walkers, runners and cyclists.

### Who?
All walking abilities, all-terrain strollers, child pack carriers.

## Bow Loop ...

### When?
Any time of day as the trail is a mix of sun and shade.

### Where?
Take Highway 1 to Exit 89, Canmore Town Center. Take the Main Street (8th Street) of Canmore and follow the signs to the Nordic Centre.  Cross over the river and take the first left into the public parking lot. There is a Boat Launch and Public Parking sign directly across from the parking lot entrance.

**Plan B** – See Page 48.

## Cougar Creek Hike – 2K Return

## What?

With a spectacular view of the Three Sisters Mountain Range, this hike winds alongside Cougar Creek. The trail is a mixture of pavement, crushed gravel and dirt, making it very suited for large wheel strollers. You can have lots of fun wading and/or throwing rocks into the creek. Approximately 700 meters from the parking lot, there is a "swimming hole" located by a large red rock: it's is a great spot to cool off on a hot day. There is no shade on the trail until approximately 770 meters from the parking lot. The Cougar Creek trail also splits into the Montane and Lady

## Cougar Creek Hike ...

McDonald trails, but these two trails are recommended for Advanced Walkers and/or children in backpack carriers: they are not stroller friendly.

### Who?
All walking abilities, all-terrain strollers, child pack carriers.

### When?
There is limited shade, so early morning or late afternoon are the best times to go.

### Where?
Take Highway 1 (One) to the Canmore Town Center, Exit 89, go east on Benchlands Trail and turn right onto Elk Run Blvd. The parking lot and trail head are just after this turn on the east side of the road.

**Plan B** – See Page 48.

# Grassi Lakes – 4K return

 *Trail Option 1*

*Trail Option 2*

## What?

The Grassi Lakes are two spectacular "mountain blue" lakes named after Lawrence Grassi, the man responsible for building the trail to them. Both lakes are very popular family picnic destinations that can be very busy on weekends and holidays. There is a narrow walking trail around both of these lakes and at the end of the second lake is a very popular climbing wall, which adds to this location's popularity.

# Grassi Lakes ...

### Who?

There are two trail options. The start for both of them is located close to the vault toilets.

*Option 1: More Difficult\*:* This interpretive trail, built by Lawrence Grassi, is best suited for advanced walkers and child pack carriers. The first part of this trail is quite gentle. However, it does get difficult with steep steps and steep cliffs closer to the top. This trail option offers stunning views of Canmore, Ha Ling Peak and the waterfall below the lakes.

*Option 2: Easy\*:* This option is for all walking abilities. This trail follows the TransAlta access road up to the lakes. The views along this trail are not as stunning as the More Difficult trail (Option 1). You still get a great view of Canmore, you can hear the waterfall and you can see Ha Ling Peak. You also can explore an old building visible from this trail.

*\*More Difficult and Easy are the designation of difficulty used at the trail head.*

### When?

Any time of day as both trail options have a mix of sun and shade.

### Where?

Take Highway 1 to the Canmore Town Center, Exit 89. Go

**Grassi Lakes ...**

west on Main (8th) Street, and follow the signs to the Nordic Centre. You will then be on Eighth Avenue. Turn north-west onto Spray Lakes Road, go past the Canmore Nordic Centre and take the first left onto a road called "Spray Lake Residences."

**Plan B** – See Page 48.

# Grotto Canyon – 5K Return

## What?

For the Canyon portion of this hike, you are walking along the creek bed, rather than on a designated trail. Being so close to Canmore, it is a popular hike for hikers and climbers, as well as our four-legged canine friends. Children love to bounce from rock to rock along the Canyon floor There are often pools of water to be manoeuvred around. The fact that there is not a designated trail to follow provides

ample opportunity for inquisitive and creative minds to create their own "adventures" as they continue to the end of the Canyon.

**Grotto Canyon ...**

**Who?**
Competent and advanced walkers, child pack carriers.

**When?**
The Canyon is shaded, but other parts of the trail are not. Go in the early morning or late afternoon, if you want to avoid the noon-time sun. Take precautions as the rocks are very slippery when wet.

**Where?**
*Option 1: Grotto Pond Day Use Area –*
This location is on Highway 1A, west of the Rafter Six cut-off on Highway 1 (One) and east of Canmore.

Follow the path from the parking lot to the start of the Canyon. This path follows the access road under the power lines. This part of the trail lacks shade. Stay on this trail, past a dry river bed until you come to a post with a red trail marker on it. Continue past the BayMag Plant #2 and look for a bench. Turn right and you will walk into the mouth of Grotto Canyon.

*Option 2: BayMag Plant #2 parking lot –*
Located on Highway 1A just west of the Grotto Pond Day Use Area, this is a more direct route to the Canyon. Parking here eliminates the first part of the trail that runs under the hydro lines. This parking lot is smaller than the Grotto Pond Day Use parking lot.

Grotto Canyon ...

## Plan B—Grotto Canyon
### • *Grotto Pond –*

A great day use area for picnics and fishing. It is located in the Grotto Pond day use parking lot. There are a few picnic tables in the shade on the edge of the pond and adjacent to the parking lot.

Other alternatives—see Page 48 for details.

## Heart Creek Trail – 3K return

### What?

This 3K hike nestles in the valley between Mount McGillivray and Heart Mountain. The pathway meanders along the creek and crosses over eight bridges ending at a rock wall. You can hear the waterfall at this point, but unless you are willing to get wet or have the ability to climb, the falls are hard to see. This hike is a popular destination for climbers, which add to the ambience of this great family hike, which is also popular with dogs and their owners.

# Heart Creek ...

## Who?

Competent and advanced walkers, child pack carriers.

## When?

Any time of day, as the trail is a mix of sun and shade.

## Where?

Take Highway 1 to the Lac Des Arc turn-off and follow the signs to the Heart Creek Trail parking lot, located on the opposite side of the road from the tiny community of Lac-Des Arc.

**Plan B** – See Page 48.

# Larch Islands Loop – 1.5 K loop

## What?

This 1.5K interpretive loop goes through a sensitive ecosystem that is home to many animals and small, moisture-loving plants. You can pick up a self-guided brochure for this trail at the Canmore Town Office, the Recreation Centre or the Library.  When you come to the end of the self-guided loop, you will exit back onto the Bow River Trail. Turn right onto this path and head back to the trail head.  Larch Park is also at this exit and is a perfect spot to reward little hikers for their efforts. Although the trail is wide enough to push a single stroller, keep in mind that you are going through a sensitive area. Try to keep on the trail with

## Larch Islands Loop ...

the stroller so you don't cause damage to the plants. Also note that after stop #5, you need to stay to the right to remain on the gravel trail.

### Who?
All walking abilities, child pack carriers, single all-terrain strollers.

### When?
Any time of day as the trail is a mix of sun and shade.

### Where?
Take Highway 1 to the Canmore Town Center, Exit 89, go west on Main (8th) Street, turn north on 7th Avenue, follow it past the pond as it goes over 8th Avenue and eventually ends at 15th Street. Continue west on 15th Street to 11th Avenue, turn north on 11th Avenue and west onto 16th Street. The trail head is at the end of this street and is visible from the left of the Bow River Trail . Or you could leave your car at Lions Park and walk to the trail head (approx. 10 min).

**Plan B** – See Page 48.

# Policeman's Creek Boardwalk – 0.8 K return

## What?

This elevated boardwalk, a popular walk in all seasons due to its proximity to downtown, takes you beside Policeman's Creek and over some marshy areas, ending at the Spring Creek condo complex. It's a great place to look for aquatic life in the marshy areas: ducks, frogs, small fish and water-loving larvae. There are many pathways throughout the town of Canmore. You can get a trail guide from the Canmore Information Center, located at 907A 7th Ave.

## Who?

All walking abilities, all-terrain strollers, child pack carriers.

## Policeman's Creek Boardwalk ...

### When?

There is limited shade, so early morning or late afternoon are the best times to go.

### Where?

Take Highway 1 to the Canmore Town Center, Exit 89, go west on Main (8th) Street. The start of this trail is located at Main (8th) Street and Spring Creek Road, across from the Big Head on Main Street. You can park anywhere along the main street or in one of the public parking lots in town.

**Plan B** – See Page 48.

# Overview of the Kananaskis Hikes

| Hike | Page | (icon 1) | (icon 2) | (icon 3) | (icon 4) | (icon 5) | (icon 6) | (icon 7) | (icon 8) | (icon 9) | (icon 10) | (icon 11) | (icon 12) | (icon 13) | (icon 14) |
|---|---|---|---|---|---|---|---|---|---|---|---|---|---|---|---|
| Barrier lake Forestry Ecology Trail (2.3k loop) | 68 | | × | | × | × | | × | | | | × | | | × |
| Boulton Creek (3k loop) | 70 | | × | | × | × | | × | | | × | × | | | × |
| Canadian Mount Everest Expedition Trail (2.3k loop) | 72 | | | | × | × | | | | | | × | | | |
| Elbow Lake (4k return) | 74 | × | | | × | × | | | | | | × | × | | × |
| Marl Lake Loop (3k return) | 76 | × | | × | × | × | | | | | | × | × | | × |
| Mount Lorette Ponds (.5k loop) | 78 | | | × | | | × | × | | | × | | × | | × |
| Rawson Lake (8k return) | 80 | × | | | × | × | | × | | | | × | | | × |

# Overview of the Kananaskis Hikes

| Hike | Page |  |  |  | 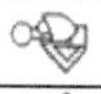 |  |  |  |  | 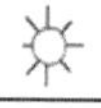 |  | 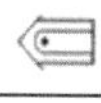 |  |  |  |
|---|---|---|---|---|---|---|---|---|---|---|---|---|---|---|---|
| Ribbon Creek Loop (4.5k return to 1st bridge) | 82 | X | | X | X | X | | X | X | | X | X | X | | |
| Sarrail Falls (3k return) | 84 | X | | | X | | | | | | X | X | X | | |
| The Rockwall (0.5k loop) | 86 | X | X | | X | | | | | | X | | X | | |
| Troll Falls (3.2k loop) | 88 | X | | | X | | | | | | X | | X | | |
| Village Rim Trail (1.5k loop) | 90 | X | X | X | X | | | | | X | | | X | | |
| Warspite lake (4.3k loop) | 92 | X | | | X | X | | | X | | X | X | | | X |
| Wedge Pond (1k loop) | 94 | X | | X | X | X | | | X | | X | X | X | | |

## Plan B – Kananaskis

### Boulton Creek Trading Post

There is a restaurant offering deli-style food, as well as ice cream. A general store is attached to this location. During the summer months, park interpreters set up exhibits about the wildlife and vegetation found within Kananaskis. Take Highway 40 south to the Kananaskis Lake Trail to the Boulton Creek Campground.

### Kananaskis Village

There is a playground located west of the parking lot and beside the tennis courts. The village also offers a deli and restaurant for meals. Take Highway 40 south to the Kananaskis Village/Nakiska turn-off. Take the first left after the bridge and follow the signs to the Kananaskis Village.

### Peter Lougheed Visitor Centre

This interpretive centre provides informative, interactive displays about the local wildlife, ecology and geology of this area. There is a great room that provides a dry, warm location to have lunch. Park staff is on hand to answer questions. There are flush toilets at this location. Take Highway 40 south to the Kananaskis Lake Trail to the Peter Lougheed Visitor Centre.

*Take a Hike ... Lynda Pianosi*

# Barrier Lake Forestry Ecology Trail
## – 2.3 K Loop

## What?

This is an easy 2.3K interpretive loop that illustrates Forest Ecology. The University of Calgary Kananaskis Field Stations and the Alberta Land and Forest Service have developed a guide for the eighteen interpretive stops along this trail. You can get a copy of this guide at the Kiosk at the start of the trail or at the Colonel's Cabin Historic Site. Some of the topics you will read about on this trail are the species of trees, the effects of fire on the forest and the types of mammals that live in the forest. Please recycle the

**Barrier Lake ...**

interpretive guide by putting it back in the kiosk so others can use it.

## Who?
All-terrain strollers, competent and advanced walkers, child pack carriers.

## When?
Any time of day as the trail is a mix of sun and shade.

## Where?
Take Highway 40 to Kananaskis Trail at the University of Calgary Kananaskis Field Station turn-off. Take your first left and park at the Colonel's Cabin parking lot.

**Plan B** – See Page 67.

# Boulton Creek – 3K Loop

## What?

This easy 3K interpretive loop takes you through a lodge-pole pine forest behind the Boulton Creek Campsites and back along Boulton Creek. The trail starts after the bridge over Boulton Creek and goes up the hill to a "retired" Fish and Wildlife Cabin. There are steep slopes along the trail behind the campsites, so this part of the trail is best suited for Competent Walkers. The lower part of this loop follows Boulton Creek and is suitable for all walking abilities.

## Who?

Competent and advanced walkers, all-terrain strollers, child

**Boulton Creek ...**

pack carriers.

**When?**
Any time of day as the trail is
a mix of sun and shade.

**Where?**
Take Highway 40 south to the
Kananaskis Trail Road and
continue to the Boulton Creek
Bridge parking lot.

**Plan B** – See Page 67.

# Canadian Mount Everest Expedition Trail – 2.3 K loop

## What?

The 2.3K interpretive loop meanders through a mature forest and ends at the top of a hill, providing spectacular views of both the Upper and Lower Kananaskis Lakes. The interpretive sign at the trail head explains that this hike is named in honour of the first 11 Canadians to conquer Mount Everest. Rest assured that the elevation gain on this hike isn't anything like the one experienced by the eleven

**Canadian Mount Everest Expedition Trail ...**

Canadian mountaineers!

The trail is wide enough in sections for a stroller, however, there are several sets of stairs that would require the stroller to be pushed or carried up. This isn't to say that it can't be done.

**Who?**
Advanced walkers, child pack carriers.

**When?**
Any time of day as the trail is a mix of sun and shade.

**Where?**
Take Highway 40 south to the Kananaskis Lake Trail and continue to the White Spruce Parking Lot. The trail head is well marked and starts at the edge of the parking lot.

**Plan B** – See Page 67.

*Take a Hike ... Lynda Pianosi*

# Elbow Lake – 4K Return

## What?

This is a steady, strenuous climb up to the crystal clear waters of Elbow Lake. Once at the lake, you can try your luck at fishing or just take in the scenery and have a picnic. For those who would still like to explore, there is a trail around the lake . This lake is also a popular back-country camping destination for families with younger children. A back-country permit is required for overnight stays here. This trail is very wide and is used by horseback riders and cyclists.

## Elbow Lake ...

### Who?

Advanced walkers (all walking abilities at the lake) , all-terrain strollers, child pack carriers.

### When?

Any time of day as the trail is a mix of sun and shade.

### Where?

Take Highway 1 to Highway 40 south past the Kananaskis Lake Trail and continue to the Elbow Pass day use parking lot.

**Plan B** – See Page 67.

## Marl Lake Loop – 3K Return

### What?

This is an easy 3K interpretive, looped trail with the highlight being Marl Lake with its spectacular Mountain Views. The interpretive portion of this trail discusses the changes to the forest, the forest life cycle and the geology of this area. There is a small dock at the lake which offers a chance to sit and watch for insects, such as dragonflies, and aquatic life, such as frogs and fish.

### Who?

All walking abilities, all-terrain strollers, child pack carriers.

## Marl Lake Loop ...

### When?
Any time of day as the trail is a mix of sun and shade.

### Where?
Take Highway 40 south to the Kananaskis Lake Trail and continue to the Elkwood Amphitheatre parking lot. From the parking lot follow the trail signs to the amphitheatre. The trail starts behind the amphitheatre and will cross the Elkwood campground roads twice. You will also come to a sign that points towards the Marl Lake Trail and Elkwood C&D loops. Continue on the trail until you see the Marl Lake Trail sign.

### Plan B – See Page 67.

*Take a Hike … Lynda Pianosi*

# Mount Lorette Ponds – 0.5K

### What?

The trail loops around a series of five ponds that are stocked with fish. It is a paved pathway, making it an ideal location for beginner walkers and for pushing strollers. It's also a great picnic spot and an ideal location for children to try their luck with the fishing rod. There are plenty of picnic tables to choose from.

### Who?

All walking abilities, all-terrain strollers, child pack carriers.

### Mount Lorette Ponds ...

**When?**
There is limited
shade, so early
mornings or
late afternoons
are the best
times to go.

**Where?**
Take Highway
1 to Highway
40 south to the

Mount Lorette Ponds turn-off, approximately five minutes
south of the Kananaskis Barrier Lake Information Centre.

**Plan B** – See Page 67.

## Rawson Lake – 8K Return

### What?

This is one of the four hikes in this book that are actually over 5K, but it is well worth it. This beautiful crystal clear lake is nestled at the base of some spectacular mountain scenery and alpine meadows. You gain a lot of elevation in the first half of this trail, but the many switchbacks make the task less daunting. The trail is best suited for advanced walkers. You can push a single all-terrain stroller but, be advised, it is a workout! The lake is stocked with fish that you can clearly see, but not always catch! (Check fishing

## Rawson Lake ...

regulations before you hike). The pikas can be seen and heard as you wander around the lake. Grizzly bears have been spotted here, so take all necessary precautions and obey all trail closure signs.

### Who?
Advanced walkers, single all-terrain strollers, and child pack carriers.

### When?
Any time of day as the trail is a mix of sun and shade.

### Where?
Take Highway 1 to Highway 40 south to the Kananaskis Lake Trail to the Upper Kananaskis Lake parking lot and day use area. Take the south side of the Kananaskis Lake Trail, past Sarrail Falls, access to the Rawson Lake Trail is on the left, after Sarrail Falls, it is clearly marked.

**Plan B** – See Page 67.

*Take a Hike ... Lynda Pianosi*

## Ribbon Creek Loop – 4.4 K return to 1st Bridge

### What?

The trail follows a flat, gravel road that once serviced the small mining community of Kovach. Ribbon Creek meanders along beside this trail. This is a great additional hike, as you can opt to hike the first 4.4k return trip to the third bridge that crosses Ribbon Creek, or if you choose, continue along the 6K loop.

### Who?

All walking abilities, all-terrain strollers, child pack carriers.

## Ribbon Creek Loop ...

### When?
Any time of day as the trail is a mix of sun and shade.

### Where?
Take Highway 1 to Highway 40 south to the Kananaskis Village/Nakiska turn-off. Take the first left after the bridge and follow the signs to the Kananaskis Village. Take the first right into the Ribbon Creek parking lot.

**Plan B** – See Page 67.

## Sarrail Falls – 3 K return

### What?

This easy trail follows the shores of Upper Kananaskis Lake to the scenic Sarrail Water Falls. The first one-quarter of the trail is in the direct sun, but the remainder of the trail is in the shade. There are many mushrooms, fungi and moisture-loving plants to see along the way. You are presented with views of Upper Kananaskis Lake and the surrounding mountains. If you choose, you can continue following this trail past the falls: it loops for 16K around Upper Kananaskis Lake.

## Sarrail Falls ...

### Who?
All walking abilities, all-terrain strollers, child pack carriers.

### When?
Any time of day as the trail is a mix of sun and shade.

### Where?
Take Highway 1 to Highway 40 south to the Kananaskis Lake Trail. Park at the Upper Kananaskis Lake parking lot and day use area.

**Plan B** – See Page 67.

# The Rockwall – 0.5 K loop

**What?**

This 0.5K paved, wheelchair accessible, interpretive loop takes you to a lookout point overlooking the Opal Range and the Rockwall Fen. A Fen is a wetland nourished by nutrient wet groundwater.

**Who?**

All walking abilities, all-terrain strollers, child pack carriers.

**When?**

Any time of day as the trail is a mix of sun and shade.

**The Rockwall ...**

**Where?**
Take Highway 1 to Highway 40 south, follow it to the
Kananaskis Lake Trail and continue to the Peter Lougheed
Visitor Centre.

**Plan B** – See Page 67.

## Troll Falls – 3.2 K loop

### What?

This easy 3.2K loop takes you along a well-worn path, through a mature aspen grove to Troll Falls and then loops back along the Hay Meadow Trail. Or you can return the same way that you came. Children will be excited by the chance to get close to the falls.

The Hay Meadow portion of this trail is a great vantage point to view (with binoculars) the Golden Eagle migration in the spring and fall months.

### Who?

All walking abilities, all-terrain strollers, child pack carriers.

### When?

Any time of day as the trail is a mix of sun and shade.

**Troll Falls ...**

**Where?**
Take Highway 1 to Highway 40 south to the Kananaskis
Village/Nakiska Ski Hill turn-off. Turn right into the Stoney
Trail Head parking lot.  Go to the other side of the metal gate
and head towards the green trail sign. The trail starts to the
left.

**Plan B** – See Page 67.

## Village Rim Trail – 1.5 K loop

### What?

This is very easy 1.5K loop around Kananaskis Village on a flat, paved pathway. The southern portion of this trail provides some amazing mountain views of Kananaskis. It is very popular loop during the summer months and an excellent one to do with very young children. There are other trails around the Kananaskis Village: you can get a trail map for these from the concierge desk in the Delta Lodge.

### Who?

All walking abilities, all-terrain strollers, child pack carriers.

### When?

There is limited shade, so early morning or late afternoon are the best times to go.

## Village Rim Trail ...

### Where?

Take Highway 1 to Highway 40 south to the Kananaskis
Village/Nakiska turn-off. Take your first left after the bridge
and follow the signs to the Kananaskis Village.

### Plan B – See Page 67.

# Warspite Lake – 4.3 K loop

## What?

This moderately easy 4.3K, interpretive loop takes you through a subalpine forest up to Warspite Lake and then takes you back to the trail head. The first quarter of the trail is a moderate uphill climb, but the remainder is relatively flat in comparison. The interesting "rock garden" that you come to before reaching Warspite Lake reminded my children of a scene from Star Wars. You can go off the trail and explore the shores of Warspite Lake, before heading back onto the forested trail and down to the parking lot.

**Warspite Lake ...**

### Who?

All walking
abilities, all-terrain
strollers, child
pack carriers.

### When?

Any time of day as
the trail is a mix of
sun and shade.

### Where?

*Option 1:* Take Highway 40 south to the Kananaskis Lake
Trail and turn onto the Smith-Dorrien/Spray Lakes Trail. The
trail head is in the parking lot for the Mount Black Prince day
use area.


*Option 2:* From Canmore, take the Smith-Dorrien/Spray
Lakes Trail to the parking lot for the Mount Black Prince day
use area.


**Plan B** – See Page 67.

*Take a Hike ... Lynda Pianosi*

## Wedge Pond – 1 K loop

### What?

This location is more of a day-use destination for fishing, picnicking and hanging out by the pond. There is however, an easy 1K loop around the pond that is ideal for All Walking Abilities. Wedge pond is also accessible by bike along the Evan Thomas Bike Path and we have often made Wedge Pond our destination when riding our bikes along this trail from the Kananaskis Village.

### Who?

All walking abilities, all-terrain strollers, child pack carriers.

**Wedge Pond ...**

**When?**
Any time of day as the trail is a mix of sun and shade.

**Where?**
Take Highway 1 to Highway 40 south to the Wedge Pond
day use area.

**Plan B** – See Page 67.

# Overview of the Lake Louise Hikes

| Hike | Page | [icon 1] | [icon 2] | [icon 3] | [icon 4] | [icon 5] | [icon 6] | [icon 7] | [icon 8] | [icon 9] | [icon 10] | [icon 11] | [icon 12] | [icon 13] | [icon 14] |
|---|---|---|---|---|---|---|---|---|---|---|---|---|---|---|---|
| Mirror Lake (5km return) | 99 | X | | | X | X | | | | | | X | X | | X |
| Lake Agnes Tea House (10 km return) | 99 | X | | | X | X | | | | | | X | X | | X |
| Lake Louise River Loop (7.1km) | 102 | | | X | X | X | | | | | | X | | | X |
| Lake Louise Shoreline (4km return) | 104 | | | X | | X | | | | | | | X | X | X |
| Larch Valley (9km return) | 106 | X | | | X | X | | | | | | X | | X | |
| Moraine Lake Shoreline (3km return) | 108 | | | X | X | X | | | | | | X | | X | X |
| The Rockpile (1.4km return) | 110 | X | | | X | | X | | | | | X | | X | |

## Plan B – Lake Louise

### *Moraine Lake Lodge*

Browse through the store. Food is offered here as well. Take Highway 1 to the Lake Louise Village turnoff, turn west onto Lake Louise Drive, go through the village and follow the signs to the Moraine Lake turn-off.

### *Chateau Lake Louise*

Visit the hotel, have lunch, buy an ice-cream and enjoy the view. Take Highway 1 to the Lake Louise village turnoff, turn west towards the village and follow the signs to Lake Louise.

### *Lake Louise Community Recreation Grounds*

This is a park that is best suited for toddlers. Take Highway 1 to the Lake Louise turn-off, turn east onto Village Drive and follow the signs to the recreation grounds.

### *Samson Mall & the Parks Canada Information Centre*

This outside mall offers gift shops, a bakery, a grocery, restaurants, and a bookstore. The Parks Canada Information Centre, located a short walk from the mall, provides information on Lake Louise and surrounding area.

## Lake Agnes Teahouse – 10 K return
## Mirror Lake – 5.2 K return

## What?

I put this 10K return hike in for those parents who feel the need for a challenge. We have pushed our All-Terrain Stroller to the stairs of the Tea House on two occasions. The first time, both children were passengers. The second time our eldest child walked three-quarters of the trail without help. It can be done! Remember, you can turn back at any time! Alternatively, you can make Mirror Lake, a 5.2K hike, your destination.  Both of these destinations are on the same trail so you can "test the waters" to Mirror Lake. You pick up the

## Lake Agnes Teahouse & Mirror Lake ...

trail just off the Lake Louise Shoreline. This is a very popular trail during the summer. If you make it to the Lake Agnes Tea House, you will be rewarded with a spectacular panoramic view of the Victoria Glacier that sits above Lake Agnes. You can also reward yourselves with home baked treats from the Lake Agnes Tea House.

### Who?
Advanced walkers (Lake Agnes Teahouse) and competent walkers (Mirror Lake) , all-terrain strollers, child pack carriers,

### When?
Any time of day as the trail is a mix of sun and shade.

### Where?
Take Highway 1 to the Lake Louise Village turnoff, turn west towards the village and follow the signs to Lake Louise.

**Plan B** - See page 98

## Lake Agnes Teahouse & Mirror Lake ...

# Lake Louise Bow River Loop – 7.1 K

## What?

This flat, wide, gravel pathway meanders along the Bow River in Lake Louise. Although the total distance is a 7.1K round trip from trail head at The Railway Station Restaurant, you can access and exit this trail at several locations, which provides the option of doing shorter portions of this hike.

## Who?

All walking abilities, all-terrain stroller, child pack carriers

## When?

Any time of day as the trail is a mix of sun and shade. A word

## Lake Louise Bow River Loop ...

of caution, there can be a lot of bear activity on this trail during berry season, late summer to early fall. Make lots of noise and obey trail closures.

### Where?

Take Highway to the Lake Louise Village turnoff, turn west onto Lake Louise Drive. Before the river turn onto Sentinel Road and follow the road to the trail head parking lot, opposite the restaurant.

**Plan B** - See page 98

# Lake Louise Shoreline – 4 K return

## What?

This wheelchair accessible trail follows the picturesque Lake Louise shoreline and offers post-card views of the Victoria Glacier. It is a very popular trail all year long, but even more so in the summer. The end of this trail is a popular spot for rock climbers.

## Who?

All walking abilities, all-terrain stroller, child pack carriers

104

**Lake Louise Shoreline ...**

**When?**
Any time of day as the trail is a mix of sun and shade.

**Where?**
Take Highway 1 to the Lake Louise Village turnoff, turn west onto Lake Louise Drive towards the village and follow the signs to the Lake Louise parking lot. Follow the signs from the parking lot to the trail head.

**Plan B** - See page 98

*Take a Hike ... Lynda Pianosi*

# Larch Valley – 9K Return

### What?

Yes another hike that is over 5K, but again it is one for the parents. This is a gorgeous hike, with many switchbacks, and a very popular fall hike as the Larch Trees, for which the hike is named, are in their full gold fall foliage. Just remember that you can turn back at any time as you know your and your children's capabilities best.

### Who?

Advanced walkers, single all-terrain stroller, child pack carriers,

## Larch Valley ...

### When?
Any time of day as the trail is a mix of sun and shade.

### Where?
Take Highway to the Lake Louise Village turnoff, turn west onto Lake Louise Drive, go through the village and follow the signs to the Moraine Lake turn-off.

**Plan B** - See page 98

*Take a Hike ... Lynda Pianosi*

# Moraine Lake Shoreline – 3K return

### What?

This is an easy walk along the Moraine Lake shoreline that offers a stunning view of the Valley of the Ten Peaks, which used to be the scene on the back of the Canadian $20.00 bill.

### Who?

All Walking Abilities, All-Terrain Stroller, Child Pack Carriers

### When?

Any time of day as the trail is a mix of sun and shade.

**Moraine Lake Shoreline ...**

**Where?**
Take Highway 1 to the Lake Louise Village turnoff, turn west onto Lake Louise Drive, go through the village and follow the signs to the Moraine Lake turn-off.

**Plan B** - See page 98

*Take a Hike ... Lynda Pianosi*

# The Rockpile – 1.4 K return

### What?

This interpretive trail, with a relatively steep set of stairs, meanders up a large glacial deposit of rocks, hence the name. Once at the top, you are rewarded with a postcard view of Moraine Lake and the Valley of the Ten Peaks.

### Who?

Advanced walkers, child pack carriers

### When?

There is limited shade, so early morning or late afternoon are

110

**The Rockpile ...**

the best times to go.  Caution should be taken if raining, because the steps and trail would be slippery when wet.

**Where?**
Take Highway 1 to the Lake Louise Village turnoff, turn west onto Lake Louise Drive, go through the village and follow the signs to the Moraine Lake turn-off.

**Plan B** - See page 98

## Big Hill Springs Provincial Park - 2K loop

**What?**

Approximately 30 minutes north/west of Calgary, this park is situated between the foothills and the grasslands. The well shaded trail meanders along a series of waterfalls and interesting geological features called Tufa's. Park signage describes Tufa's as "a rock that forms when calcium and carbonate rich water emerges from the ground. As the water comes to the surface, it releases carbon dioxide into the air and forms the calcium carbonate rock called Tufa." It is also the site of an historic fish hatchery and Alberta's first

### Big Hill Springs Provincial Park ...

commercial creamery.  This is a very popular destination for families and dog walkers, and over time, informal side-trails have been created off of the main trail.  Help reduce the negative impact these side trails have made on the area, and stick to the main trail.

### Who?
All-terrain strollers, child pack carriers, competent walkers

### When?
Any time of day as the trail is a mix of sun and shade.

### Where?
Coming from Calgary take, Highway 1A west to Secondary road 766 North, continue to Secondary Road 567 West, also called Big Hill Springs Road. Continue west until you come to Big Hill Springs Trial.  Follow this paved road to the parking lot.

# Glenbow Ranch Provincial Park

## What?

Located 15 minutes west of Calgary, this park consists of 35 k of paved and gravel trails that meander along the Bow River, and pass through coulees, grasslands and significant cultural and historical features, in addition, many of these trails offer a panoramic view of the mountains. The Harvie family donated the land for this park, for which they were honoured with the Nature Conservancy of Canada Alberta Order of Conservation. The park's interpretive center, the Harvie's homestead, provides educational and historical information on the park. Park interpreters are on-hand to answer any questions, and in the summer months, provide a variety of

## Glenbow Ranch Provincial Park ...

guided tours. For more information regarding the tours, go to www.grpf.ca.

### Who?

All-terrain strollers, child pack carriers, competent walkers

### When?

There is limited shade on the trails, early morning of late afternoon would be best.

### Where?

Highway 1A west to Cochrane, turn south (left) at Glenbow Road. This 2.8 km gravel road will take you to the parking lot.

## About the Author—Lynda Pianosi

Lynda Pianosi is the mother of two sons. Together with her husband Doug, she and the family have been hiking since her oldest son was 10 months old. She searched in vain for a book that offered 5K and under hikes that she could do with her family. There wasn't one!

That's when Lynda's research turned practical. They started with easy hikes that would work with their Chariot. These included the Fenland Trail in Banff, Troll Falls in Kananaskis and the Lake Louise Shoreline. Through trial and error, as they tried some hikes mentioned in other books, they found the ones that worked best for their family. Lynda and her family have been on every hike in this book more than once.

Passionate about getting their children out of the house

and active in the fresh outdoors, Lynda and Doug have used all methods for taking their children out on the trail, including all-terrain strollers, child pack carriers and bribery. For days when none of these worked, Plan B was born. Her children, the best critics of all, have approved all the hikes and Plan Bs in her book.

Lynda and Doug live in Canmore and hike whenever the seasons allow. They have reintroduced hiking to many of their friends with children the same age as their own.

Lynda is passionate about the environment and wants her children and others to understand how plants, animals and people are interconnected.

You may contact Lynda at
Pianosi Publishing,
Box 8329
Canmore AB, T1W 2V1
Email: Lynda@takeahikewithyourchildren.ca
www.takeahikewithyourchildren.ca

THREE MOUNTAIN
FAMILY
HIKES

*Getting families*
*closer to nature*
*one step at a time*